Norbert's
LITTLE LESSONS
FOR A BIG LIFE

JULIE STEINES *and* VIRGINIA FREYERMUTH

Photography by MARK STEINES

NORTH STAR WAY

New York   London   Toronto   Sydney   New Delhi

North Star Way
An Imprint of Simon & Schuster, Inc.
1230 Avenue of the Americas
New York, NY 10020

First North Star Way hardcover edition October 2017

NORTH STAR WAY and colophon are trademarks of Simon & Schuster, Inc.

For information about special discounts for bulk purchases,
please contact Simon & Schuster Special Sales at
1-866-506-1949 or business@simonandschuster.com.

The North Star Way Speakers Bureau can bring authors to your live event. For more information or to book an event, contact the North Star Way Speakers Bureau at 1-212-698-8888 or visit our website at www.thenorthstarway.com.

Interior design by Jaime Putorti

Manufactured in the United States of America

10 9 8 7 6 5 4 3 2 1

Library of Congress Cataloging-in-Publication Data is available.

ISBN 978-1-5011-8731-5
ISBN 978-1-5011-8733-9 (ebook)

THIS BOOK IS DEDICATED TO THE NORBERTHOOD.

YOU ARE MY FRIENDS FOREVER,

NORBERT

Norbert's

LITTLE LESSONS

FOR A BIG LIFE

HI!

I'M NORBERT!

WELCOME TO THE NORBERTHOOD,
A PLACE OF KINDNESS AND COMPASSION.
I'M GLAD YOU'RE HERE.

SOME PEOPLE SAY I'M A LITTLE DOG.
AT JUST 7 INCHES TALL, I SUPPOSE THAT'S TRUE,
BUT I HAVE A VERY BIG HEART.

I was born in California in 2009, the only puppy in my litter. I'm a mixed-breed: Chihuahua, Cairn Terrier, and Lhasa Apso. That makes me a one-of-a-kind dog.

When I was four months old, Julie Steines (formerly Julie Freyermuth) adopted me through PetFinder. I was not in a shelter or rescue, but due to my tiny size, I needed a special home. I was just a wee puff of brown fur at the time. I traveled to Boston to live with Julie, my new mom.

Julie said she knew I was special the minute we met and immediately noticed I had a special gift for making people smile just by being myself. She named me Norbert. Over time, my nicknames became Norbie, Norbster, and Monkey.

So Julie and I began our happily ever after together. . . .

Within a few months, Julie and I were in a local eyeglass store in Boston, and the woman working behind the counter saw me and mentioned that I would make a wonderful therapy dog. Julie didn't know what a therapy dog was or how important they were in helping people. After some research, we learned that therapy animals are trained and registered to provide love and comfort to people in need at places like hospitals, nursing homes, schools, hospices, disaster areas, and more.

Julie trained me herself, and she told me I was very smart and loving. At age one, I passed the tests and became a registered therapy dog. We started volunteering at a children's hospital and at a nursing home. I enjoyed making people smile by doing some of my fun moves, like High-Five, Zen (lie down), Tourner (turn), Namaste (stay), and Love (paw).

Over time, my fur gradually changed to white with touches of gray. That was a surprise to us both. But I never grew to be a big dog.

Everyone who helps me spread smiles is part of the Norberthood—a growing group of more than 1.5 million people worldwide who follow me on social media. I'm grateful for all our friends and so happy that my work brings joy to people around the world. It does my heart good to know that I raise awareness for other therapy animals and for pet adoption, too. You can read more about me at www.Norberthood.com.

I believe your every little thought, word, and deed can make a BIG difference in the world.

I WROTE SOME WORDS OF WISDOM,
AND I'M EXCITED TO SHARE THEM WITH YOU.

LET'S GET COMFY.

I ALSO MADE US SOME SNACKS.

LET'S BEGIN!

ATTITUDE IS EVERYTHING.

BE POSITIVE,

EVEN WHEN IT'S A STRETCH.

ALWAYS COUNT YOUR BLESSINGS,

BIG AND SMALL.

SMILE EVEN WHEN YOU'RE BLUE.

BE A SILLYBERT SOMETIMES.

IT'S FUN TO MAKE SOMEONE GIGGLE.

FIND SOMEONE TO LOOK UP TO.
AND I DON'T JUST MEAN SOMEONE TALL.

BE SURE TO OPEN THE DOOR
WHEN OPPORTUNITY KNOCKS.

TAKE A DEEP BREATH.

INHALE THE BEAUTY OF LIFE.

DO YOU KNOW YOU'RE A DEER?

OOPS. I MEAN A DEAR.

THERE ARE A WHOLE LOT OF CHOICES.

SO ALWAYS MAKE GOOD ONES.

YOU ARE WONDERFUL

JUST THE WAY YOU ARE.

MOVE YOUR PAWS WHENEVER YOU CAN.

IT'S FUN TO MAKE FUR FLY.

ARGH, MATEY.
YOU CAN BE WHOEVER
YOU WANT TO BE.
DON'T LET ANYONE TELL
YOU OTHERWISE.

CHIN UP.

SOMETIMES THE BEST STUFF

IS JUST AHEAD.

PUNS MAKE PEOPLE SMILE!

I'M SORRY. I WAS *STAIRING* AT YOU.

YOU ARE CAPTIVATING.

SPEND TIME WITH MOTHER NATURE.

CARE FOR THE PLANET WE ALL SHARE.

IT'S OUR COMMON GROUND.

A GOOD FRIEND CAN HELP YOU

TWINKLE AND SHINE.

BE THANKFUL FOR
EACH DELICIOUS MOMENT,
AND KNOW THAT THEY'RE
HELPING YOU BE STRONG.

EVERYONE SHOULD HAVE

A SPECIAL PLACE TO GO.

THINK BEFORE WAGGING

YOUR TONGUE.

YOUR BARK CAN BE

BADDER THAN YOUR BITE.

YOU'RE A SPECIAL CREATURE.

YOU CAN MAKE MAGIC HAPPEN.

ALWAYS REMEMBER,

IT'S COOL TO BE KIND.

'NUFF SAID.

NEED A PICK-ME-UP?

TWO WORDS: *POLKA DOTS.*

MAKE TIME TO DREAM.
JAMMER JAMS AND A
SOFT BLANKIE CAN HELP.

WHEN YOUR ENTHUSIASM

GETS DAMPENED,

JUST SHAKE IT OUT.

TAKE TIME TO REFLECT.
YOU JUST MIGHT SEE
THINGS MORE CLEARLY.

THINK ABOUT WHAT
YOU'RE THINKING ABOUT.
WHEN YOU CHANGE YOUR THOUGHTS,
YOU CAN CHANGE YOUR LIFE.

HELP OTHERS FIND THEIR HAPPY.

I'M ALWAYS WONDERING,

"HOW CAN I MAKE YOU SMILE?"

IF THINGS DON'T FEEL ROSY,

FOCUS ON THE BLOSSOMS,

NOT THE THORNS.

WHEN THE WORLD FEELS COLD,
FIND WAYS TO WARM THE HEART.
WE CAN ALL USE A LITTLE LOVE.

HANG OUT IN THE FIELD
OF INFINITE POSSIBILITIES
AND IMAGINE GREAT STUFF.
THAT SOUNDS GOOD.

INTENT LISTENING IS AN ART.
YOU HAVE TO OPEN YOUR EARS
AND YOUR HEART.

LIFE IS A TEAM SPORT.
WE'RE ALL IN IT TOGETHER.
BRING YOUR BEST SELF
TO EVERY GAME.

THERE'S NOTHING LIKE
A WARM BUBBLE BATH TO SOAK
YOUR CARES AND STRESS AWAY.
A SMILING DUCKIE HELPS, TOO.

CUDDLE UP.

IT FEELS GOOD.

THERE ARE MIRACLES ALL AROUND US.

THERE'S A BRIDGE BETWEEN
THE PAST AND THE FUTURE.
IT'S CALLED THE PRESENT. ENJOY IT.

BE CURIOUS.

LEARN TO LOVE LEARNING.

I MAY HAVE A LITTLE NOGGIN,

BUT IT STILL HOLDS A LOT.

SING EVEN IF IT SOUNDS LIKE BARKING.

MUSIC IS GOOD FOR THE SOUL.

AHOY!

IT TAKES A BREEZE TO SET SAIL.

WINDS OF CHANGE CAN CARRY YOU

TO NEW HORIZONS.

HAVE A WHALE OF A TIME!

I'M FLUFFY AND I LOVE BEING FLUFFY.

FIND WHAT YOU LOVE ABOUT YOURSELF,

AND DO YOU!

CREATE AND CULTIVATE
CONNECTIONS WITH OTHERS.
FRIENDS COME IN ALL SHAPES,
SIZES, AND PATTERNS.

HANG OUT WITH FRIENDS

WHO MAKE YOU LAUGH AND

HELP YOU ENJOY LIFE.

SMILE AND ENJOY THE RIDE.
HOW YOU MOVE THROUGH
LIFE IS AS IMPORTANT
AS WHERE YOU'RE HEADED.

BE ADVENTUROUS.

THAT'S HOW I ROLL.

HUG MORE OFTEN.

IT FEELS GOOD TO BE HUGGED.

IT FEELS GOOD TO GIVE A HUG.

FOLLOW YOUR HEART.
IT WILL LEAD YOU DOWN
THE MOST BEAUTIFUL PATHS.

STOP AND REST.

WHEN YOU'RE WELL RESTED,

YOU'LL BE READY FOR ANYTHING.

BE CREATIVE.

MAKE WHAT MAKES YOU HAPPY.

IF I HAD HUGE KNITTING NEEDLES,

I'D MAKE A BIG PUFFY THING

LIKE THIS.

FIND THE FUN IN EVERYDAY THINGS.

STEP IN A PUDDLE,

SPLASH AROUND,

GRIN. REPEAT.

GIVE MORE OFTEN.

THERE CAN BE A LOT OF LOVE

IN A LITTLE GIFT.

TRUST ME.

PRACTICE GRATITUDE.

IT CHANGES EVERYTHING.

YOU DON'T NEED TO BE BIG
TO MAKE A BIG DIFFERENCE
IN THE WORLD.
LET'S SPREAD SMILES TOGETHER.

BYE FOR NOW.

YOU ARE MY FRIEND FOREVER.

⸂ WAYS I MAKE A DIFFERENCE ⸃

Making others smile is the most rewarding thing to me. It's something everyone can do, so I hope my work inspires you to find ways to be thoughtful and kind. Here are some favorite memories of ways I've made others smile:

• As a registered therapy dog, when I visit children's hospitals with Julie, it gives me so much joy to see a child's face light up when we come into the room.

• I visited families at an inner-city homeless shelter where I gave high fives during a holiday celebration and made people of all ages smile.

• I went on a road trip to surprise a woman who was in the hospital getting a chemotherapy treatment on her birthday. The look on her face was priceless; it was a touching visit I will never forget.

• I traveled by plane to visit a brave young boy who was battling cancer.

• I helped coordinate a trip for a little boy with a rare disease so that we could hang out together and have some fun.

• I helped raise thousands of dollars for an organization to benefit homeless pets with special needs.

∽ CHARITIES I SUPPORT ∽

In addition to my own charitable work, I also love supporting a variety of organizations and nonprofits that are doing good work in the world. Here are a few of my favorites:

Amerman Family Foundation Dog Therapy Program at Children's Hospital Los Angeles
www.CHLA.org/DogTherapy
www.CHLA.org/GiveToDogTherapy

For donations:
4650 Sunset Blvd #170
Los Angeles, CA 90027
(323) 361-6580

Marine Toys for Tots®
www.toysfortots.org
Marine Toys for Tots Foundation
18251 Quantico Gateway Dr.
Triangle, VA 22172
(703) 640-9433

Best Friends Animal Society
bestfriends.org
5001 Angel Canyon Road
Kanab, UT 84741
(435) 644-2001

ᕦ A LITTLE MORE ABOUT LITTLE ME ᕤ

Julie and her mother, Virginia Freyermuth, wondered what it must feel like to be such a little dog in a great big city. This inspired the idea for our first children's picture book, *Norbert: What Can Little Me Do?* Julie and Virginia believed that my story of becoming a therapy dog and finding my special gift of making people smile would make a beautiful book. Creating the book took three years, but once it was published, our book went on to win nine prestigious book awards and became the first book in a series. In addition to this book, Julie and her mom have published two other books in our series: Norbert: *What Can Little You Do?* and *Norbert & Lil BUB: What Can Little We Do?*

In 2016, we created my own life-size Norbert plush toy, which is part of a kindhearted project I named Norberthood For Good. For every plush Norbert purchased, I donated one to Toys for Tots®, where it was given to a child in need.

My mom and I volunteer at Children's Hospital Los Angeles and continue to make special personal visits by request.

I've won recognition (blush, blush) from American Humane Hero Dog Awards, the Webby Awards, and *People* magazine. I've been lucky to further our mission to make people smile on television shows such as *Home & Family*, *The Doctors*, and *Harry* with Harry Connick Jr., among others.

◡ MEET MY MOM AND COAUTHOR, JULIE STEINES ◡

Julie is not only my mom, she's my best friend forever. We do so many heartwarming things together!

I'm humbled that, because of me, she met her husband, Mark Steines, when we appeared on *Home & Family*, the television show he cohosts. It was like a fairy tale—love at first sight. They married a year later, and I got three great new big brothers, Mark's sons, Kai and Avery, and Fred, their golden retriever. Fred is my best buddy, and our parents like to take photos of us having fun together. Now I'm a big brother to my new little sister, Parker Rose, who was born in July 2017.

Julie and I are committed to philanthropic work and to doing all we can to make the world a better place for people and animals. We volunteer our time meeting with children and adults who need a reason to smile. My mom says it's the most rewarding work of her life.

We like making appearances at charity events and were featured on a New York runway in 2016 during Fashion Week, walking in Anthony Rubio's show to bring awareness to pet adoption. Julie and I have shared our mission on the television shows *The Doctors*, *Harry*, and the Hallmark Channel's *Home & Family*. You can read about our mission in magazines and in online articles, including *People*, *Time*, *Us Weekly*, *Focus*, *Angeleno*, *Wag*, *Brides*, and many more. I've even been a celebrity guest at CatCon (where most of the cats were bigger than me).

My mom works hard every day to help me make others smile around the world on my social media platforms, Facebook.com/NorbertDog, Instagram.com/norbertthedog, and Twitter @NorbertDog.

My Mom graduated from Ohio Wesleyan University and is a member of the Phi Beta Kappa Society. She has been the co-owner of Polly Parker Press, LLC, for seven years along with her mom, Dr. Virginia Freyermuth. Through Polly Parker Press, we have published books, donated financial assistance, helped with fund-raising, and provided in-kind donations to numerous nonprofit organizations. I lucked out getting Julie for my mom, and I let her know it every day by making her smile.

✎ MEET MY COAUTHOR AND JULIE'S MOM, ✎
VIRGINIA K. FREYERMUTH, MFA, PʜD

I call Virginia by her nickname, Ginger. She has a passion for doing all kinds of creative work as an artist, writer, and teacher. An award-winning certified K–12 art educator, she received her Bachelor of Fine Arts degree and Master of Fine Arts degree in Painting. I can't tell you how many paintings she has done of me as illustrations for our picture books! She likes to capture my many moods because she tells me I'm expressive. I have sat patiently on her big drawing table in her barn studio many times so she could look closely at my face.

Ginger has been a holistic art educator for more than forty years. She has taught art to all age levels, from kindergarten through high school, college, and adults. She was humbled to be named the 1994 Massachusetts Teacher of the Year, and the 1995 Outstanding Art

Teacher of the Walt Disney American Teacher Awards. She has given more than 300 public presentations and works tirelessly as an advocate for the arts. She was a chapter author for the peer-reviewed book *The Heart of Art Education: Holistic Approaches to Creativity, Integration, and Transformation*. Ginger also has a PhD in Interdisciplinary Studies with a Concentration in Art Education.

She has prepared new art teachers for the profession in Massachusetts and Rhode Island, and was awarded the 2014 Rhode Island Higher Education Art Educator of the Year Award. She is the co-owner of Polly Parker Press, working closely with Julie. She also owns an online art school where she offers art instruction to people around the world. She believes everyone has the capacity to be creative. She says her greatest accomplishment is being a mom to her son, my uncle, Jeff, and to her daughter, Julie. She lives in Massachusetts with her husband, Richard. You can view her art portfolio and read more on her website at www.VirginiaFreyermuth.com.

～ MEET MY DAD AND PERSONAL PHOTOGRAPHER, ～
MARK STEINES

My dad, a three-time Emmy Award winner, cohosts the Hallmark Channel's Emmy-nominated *Home & Family* with Debbie Matenopoulos. In 2017, my dad, along with Leeza Gibbons, took over as hosts of KTLA's Rose Parade broadcast. He grew up in a small town in Iowa, and attended the University of Northern Iowa on a full football scholarship, graduating with a degree in Radio and Television. He ended up in Hollywood to set the gold standard in entertainment news while working at *Entertainment Tonight* for more than seventeen years.

My dad is also an actor and has guest starred on television shows such as *CSI: NY*, *The Practice*, and *America's Next Top Model*. He earned a degree from Joanne Baron/D.W.

Brown Studio's Meisner technique training. He also studied comedy at the Groundlings, the renowned school of improv. I think he's very funny and has a great sense of humor.

My dad receives rave reviews for his photography work, which encompasses portraits, landscapes, and photo journalism. His photo book, *See The Light: A Passage to Sierra Leone*, raised awareness for fresh water in impoverished countries by documenting a trip of the Light House Medical Mission in 2009. His professional photo assignments have included shooting more than thirty celebrities for Bootcampaign.org's patriotic image campaign; and editorial work for magazines including *Angeleno*, *Closer*, *Focus*, *Paper*, *Casual Living*, *The Wag*, *Animal Wellness*, *Groomer to Groomer*, and *Life After 50*, among others.

Mark's a great dad. A born fitness enthusiast, he was featured in *People* magazine's coveted "Sexiest Man Alive" issue and *Men's Fitness* magazine's "25 Fittest Men in America." My dad is also an avid hands-on, do-it-yourself kind of guy.

I think he's inspiring and lots of fun to be around. He makes me smile, which is particularly good when he has a camera in his hand!

⌒ ACKNOWLEDGMENTS ⌒

'm so grateful for the opportunity to inspire kindness through my book.

A big thank-you to my dad, Mark Steines, for the many great photographs of little me. My brothers, Kai, Avery, and Fred Steines, were a big help, too! Much love to my new baby sister, Parker Rose.

Of course, I couldn't have done this without my dear coauthors, Julie and Virginia. Hugs to my Uncle Jeff and Julie's dad, Richard, for their enthusiasm.

Thank you to Hope Diamond for finding ways to spread my message and strengthen my mission. High fives to Dr. Patrick Mahaney, my holistic veterinarian, for keeping me healthy, and to my groomer, Michael Rogers, for always making me look snappy.

A special thank-you to the entire North Star Way team and to my caring editor, Diana Ventimiglia. The enthusiasm of everyone there made the creation of this book a joy.

Last, but by no means least, to my entire family and many friends around the world, thank you for your generous hearts and the amazing ways you inspire me every day.